SOLOMON. . . .(REVISITED)

Books By

ANDERSON

ARTWORK BY

ARTWORK INSPIRED BY
MUSTAVE DORE'

SOLOMON...(REVISITED)

Anderson

authorHOUSE®

AuthorHouse™
1663 Liberty Drive
Bloomington, IN 47403
www.authorhouse.com
Phone: 1-800-839-8640

First published by AuthorHouse 5/20/2010

ISBN: 978-1-4490-7538-5 (e)
ISBN: 978-1-4490-7036-6 (sc)

Library of Congress Control Number: 2010900106

Printed in the United States of America
Bloomington, Indiana

This book is printed on acid-free paper.

ABOUT THE COVER

When I first joined the U.S.Navy in the fall of 1970, I decided, like most sailors, that I wanted a tattoo. I did not have a clue what I wanted, I just knew that I wanted something. It could not just be body art, it had to have a message. It had to say something and mean something.

Life has a tendency to take us to those places that we will not willingly go to on our own. You know the place. The place that defines who we really are.

For my fifty–sixth birthday, I finally broke down and purchased my only tattoo. For thirty–nine years, I waited for the perfect tattoo for me. The cover of this book is a re–creation of that monumental moment when all of the pieces of the puzzle finally came together.

The angel represents Gods' human creation–Man. The struggle between good and evil is represented by the Demon in the fire and the angels' halo in his right hand. We are in a tug of war with good and evil. The fiery sword in the left hand represents the battle that we are engaged in everyday of our lives.

The name "Anderson" appears on the belt of the Angel.

After a lengthy battle with the Demons of the past, I broke through to a marvelously peaceful revelation–Hence ROMANS 9:20

Can the clay say to the potter, "Why have you made me this way?"

CREDITS

In order to appropriately introduce you to this book, please let me first, introduce to you the two inspirations that have made the spirit of God come to life in this book. Because of the influence of these two, I have a better relationship with God and a greater peace than I had ever dreamed possible.

First, always and most, I thank God for the Holy Ghost and the comfort that has come with it in my old age. Without God, there is nothing. How strongly those words come off the pages in these writings. It is in, by, and for Him, that we live, and breathe and have our being.

Next, I want to thank Solomon for the inspiration for a lifetime. Solomon's wisdom has sustained me for these five decades that I have lived on the earth. Thank you again, Solomon, for a consultation with destiny. It has been a most wonderful ride.

Introduction

Life has a tendency to deal each of us hands, that sometimes, we would like to fold and wait for the next one to come along. Not very long ago, I decided to quit folding and start playing the cards that I had been dealt. Understand now, every hand has not been a winner. Sometimes, it is mind–boggling the cards that I am dealt and what I see. There have been however, some really great hands, that started out mundane. Little did I know that with those hands, I was being closely watched by God. Without my knowledge, the "Dealer" had already stacked the deck in my favor.

During the early winter of my life, I found a ray of sunshine under a rock; my head. As I poured my heart into the book that you now hold in your hands, I decided to pass on the years of education that God has allowed me to possess in order to lighten the load of someone else. These writings are in no way intended to detract from the writings of Solomon nor are they a complete work. The fact is, my hope is to add some flavor and ease of understanding to what Solomon had already done, in my own unique way.

The word says that there is nothing new under the sun. This therefore, is not a new thing either. It is merely an avenue of expression from a divine prospective that is intended to assist in our daily walk through this life.

The sonnets and poetry contained herein are an ongoing work that affords me release from the daily stresses of life. At those moments of inspiration, I cannot withhold my pen. My hope and intent is that by it, someone can catch a glimpse of the awesome power that is available within each of us if we can but follow our God–given, God–directed passions.

Even if you are not someone who likes poetry, that is alright. There are some solid and sound lessons buried within these writings that will help express how some of us actually feel and think inside but, heretofore, have been afraid to let anyone see. The sonnets contain some powerful concepts that will ring true in every life, no matter what your social or economic status may be.

Each selection is fashioned after the biblical accounts that Solomon himself, portrayed in his writings. The Proverbs (a book of wisdom for living), The Song of Solomon (a passionate love story) and Ecclesiastes (the results of a lifelong search for truth) are books in the bible attributed to Solomon. Each sonnet rings true with some of the wisdom that is available to "whosoever will."

Another idea that is presented here is one of future events. It may not necessarily be prophetic, but it does lean toward tomorrow. We can only live one day at a time but, if we cannot see where tomorrow is going, we cannot align ourselves today.

Though I am not perfect in my approach to this wisdom, I am sure that you will agree that God has influenced these writings.

Take a trip with me and let's revisit some of the wisdom of the wisest man that ever lived…..Solomon (Revisited)

Solomon presents as a powerful image in the pages of your bible. The things that he learned were beyond his years and yet, for his writings, he paid his dues. Softly layered in between every line of all three of his books is a subtle but true message. If I could glean one thing in life that would serve better than gold, it would be to live out the Proverbs of Solomon in a way that would truly bring honor and glory to God.

SOLOMON (REVISITED)

Solomon's wisdom, renown of mankind, has for centuries, enlightened mortal man.
To enlighten and reveal, was the ever resounding scope of a divine and holy plan.

Upon the hearts, upon the minds and upon the souls of an ever–growing humanity, Wisdom is
poured into the lives of men, praying for love, peace and much more sanity.

Every person alive today, yearns for much more sense for their direction,
Careful always to listen, and yet they jump at the first thing by, making their election.

Wisdom is elusive, it ever tries to hide, it even gets rejected
By the simple few who cannot understand, and thereby, are not selected.

Just grab on tight, and let the power of wisdom cause you to spiritually arise,
To that place of holy splendor, where to your contemporaries, you may appear as wise.

Living fully, all that you understand, and what your eyes will let you see,
So by it, you may apply wisdom to the life you live and believe that you can be free.

The heavy price that wisdom will require of every living creature,
Is intended, that in our daily lives, all of wisdom be completely featured.

Not just verbal fodder, or even the knowledge that wisdom does possess.
But that through its passionate truth, we live this life with true success.

The power that wisdom provides to the novice, is destructive and is cold.
But will, in the hands of a righteous man, save many a lost and dying soul.

When the twilight years have at long last, happened upon mortal man,
Will wisdom have completed her work and redeemed a helpless, hopeless land?

Will we finally apply the power of wisdom to our waning earthly lives down here,
Or will we ignore it fully and let the earth totally erupt in dread and awful fear.

     Solomon spent a great deal of time writing about the importance of the relationship between a father and his son. He ardently addresses the position granted to the male of the species. Listen to the words of the father. Listen as the father pours himself into the heart of his son for the task at hand. Training, pleading, pulling on the heart of his seed. "Listen son, I will save you heartache. I will make you wise. Listen to my lessons and learn of me." Wisdom is the principle thing. Therefore, get wisdom. Passing that wisdom to his offspring, is a Daddy's Job.

DADDY'S JOB

A daddy has an awesome task to fill, for a man just out of his teens,
Young and strapping, full of zeal and barely able to fill his own jeans.

When his firstborn child finally arrives on this old blue and green planet,
Daddy has to trap the boy inside, and for her future now, he must plan it.

Beyond the scope of being for his whole family, its main and spiritual provider,
Is an intense sense of the spirit, that is also growing now inside of her.

His desire is to see that all she wants and needs, by his own hands is there,
But much deeper still, is his obligation to God, and he places her in His care.

Trusting God, and showing still, that what he does is always worth so much,
He must provide the cover for his family; for their spirit; eternity and such.

So the pressures of life now, squeezing hard upon his tired and aching chest,
Press him on to God, where in Him alone, the boy can find that peaceful rest.

Only now, as he reaches past his prime, does he really begin to clearly see,
What his job has always been, and what his little girl, was truly meant to be.

Feeling failure, and the greatness of loss, for the things he failed to do,
He worries that he has marked for life, the same failures in her life, too.

Hope for him diminishes now, into a cloud filled with desperate gloom,
Until his child, has a child, and the light of it, begins to fill the room.

A daddy's heart is now renewed, and life for him becomes filled with cheer,
By planting in his grandchild, he can redeem what to him, has become most dear.

A daddy's job is of the most serious sort, when compared to our daily chores,
For daddy's job for his family, is to make available, and open, spiritual doors.

The thing that he must leave behind, when he crosses Jordan's' muddy river,
Is his tender heart in his offspring, as flaming arrows, from his quiver.

     Recognizing the need for a creed to live by, man searches everyday for what to him should already be real. In the heart of every man, there is a need to know God. Finding peace with the creator is a difficult task for some. Still others find solace early on and learn to live in peace with it. It becomes second nature, *first*. Therefore, find a creed that speaks from your own heart and hold its truth for life. In the end, you will have something that you can live by.

TO LIVE BY

Solomon was a man, concerned all of his life with truly knowing,
Living every day with determination, checking where he was going.

Near the end of his time, he collected his thoughts, all about real living,
Completed his thoughts, and wrote them all down, completely about wholly giving.

The whole duty of man, was to honor God and by his life, bring Him glory.
And according to Solomon, that was it, the end of the whole bible story.

A little more now to be added, for a more clear visuals sake,
If not performed from a pure heart, it will be seen as totally fake.

The test of our lives, that will be seen as real truth, from our own lips,
Will be seen by all, and a record will be kept of all our failing slips.

The record that will be kept, will be held by mortal men,
But the real record is forgiveness, and will be saved for the end.

So live your life, in pure and holy truth, with every day you have,
And the Comforter will, to all of your wounds, apply His holy salve.

Your duty to God, has been fully written, and now spiritually noted,
So do what is right always, and by no one ever be goaded.

Rest therefore, in knowing that you have done all that you truly know to do,
And when you stand before Him, you will appear as happy, not blue.

Remember always, that is before God, that you will ultimately be judged,
So do what is right always, and never ever, by any other human be budged.

Wisdom provides a rough road for those who seek her. She is often found at great cost. She has much to give and her value cannot be measured. Being able to glean from a source as valuable as wisdom will require walking where others are afraid to go. The calling is higher and the way is fraught with danger. But there is a special grace for those who see the value of a road less traveled.

A ROAD LESS TRAVELED

The Via Doloroso, where Jesus had to walk to his own end,
Is the way of suffering, that is still trodden daily by mortal men.

It is a road that still leads to hallowed sacred fame,
But only when through this life, you have left behind a gracious name.

It is a rough road that is truly feared by those who hope to win,
But, for the victors' crown, must be traveled, all the way to the very end.

It is the road less traveled, a road traveled by only a chosen few,
People with a divine purpose, armed only with what they know they must do.

The path is fraught with danger, perils and heartbreaks real,
To the vast majority, the Via Doloroso, does not have much appeal.

The rewards of this arduous way, are not often realized here below,
Because it is so rough, it is often shunned, with serious dreadful woe.

But walk down it slowly, the specially chosen must surely do,
And to their own hearts, they must always, be ever totally true.

To live life long and realize the unique and holy inspired call,
The chosen will surely go, and through His grace, will accomplish all.

So receive the problems, the tests, the hard lessons, He has designed,
Give yourself completely over, to a holy, completely humble mind.

So that the will of Him in every life, will at the end be revealed,
When down the Via Doloroso, to man and God, we have been completely real.

     Man's life is presently somewhere near the biblical edit of threescore and ten. This is granted to us on a twenty–four hour clock. We are required live it one day at a time. There are no promises for tomorrow lest you count the eternal. Giving each new day its full attention, can ease a troubled mind. But, remember this, if you do not seize the day at hand, you will miss the entire divine plan. God gave us the next twenty–four hours to seize the day.

CARPE' DIEM

Life is so short, measured by a stick called time.
Threescore and ten, and that, provided you walk the line.

Given the chances, of accomplishing your whole life's' goal,
Will cost you all you have, excluding your mortal soul.

So what would you get, if your whole life you surrendered,
If love, hope and peace, you always fostered and tendered.

The rewards that you seek, in this life cannot be found,
Unless you pick up the soul that is lost and way down.

But to know and to grasp, the awesome brevity of life,
Will make you take stock, and count your blessings without strife.

Seize the moment; seize the day; that is the heavenly call,
Live while you can fully, live for today and that is all.

The promise that we are given, includes only this day,
So give it fully to someone else is all I can truly say.

For it is in giving completely, that we truly will receive,
Carpe Diem, seize the day and always wholly believe,

That what we give and pass along to others every day,
Will return to us, pressed down and running over, in every way.

If only this day were all that we had ever been given,
Let us give it away, and that will be real godly living.

Everyone needs a special place where they can go and relax and spend some quality time with God. Life deals cards fast and hard. Sometimes, catching the right cards may come easy. But, playing them correctly can be quiet a different story. If you cannot think the hand through, then you may wind up playing the wrong card at the wrong time. Think about it. Unless a man can shrink away to a place of peace and tranquility and collect his connectedness, life will surely overtake him before his time. If you live long on this earth, you will soon learn the importance of a quiet place.

THE IMPORTANCE OF A QUIET PLACE

The spirit of man is troubled, much by the weight of each new day,
Finding a place to release that load, is important to mankind in every way.

The worries we carry and the stress we embrace, leaves us loaded and often weary.
When we are around loved ones and friends, of us, they can become very leery.

But by divine plan, we have been graced, to unload our heavy souls,
If we will find that quiet place, where the peace like a river flows.

There is a place where true peace and harmony abound,
If we look for it and in it we will live, never by stress, will we be found.

Call it quiet time or call time alone with your precious God,
Whichever it is, there you will find that tranquility does trod.

It is there in our rest, that true harmony with nature and with man,
Would be experienced fully, and pressure will release on the right and left hand.

Then with wings of peace, we may safely again, enter the mainstream,
Spreading all of the peace and harmony we've gathered, like angels in a wonderful dream.

The world is full of the hurried and fast–paced, which leaves us all just whipped.
But, by finding a quiet place, we can give the blues a sure and subtle slip.

There is no shame in running to hide, in a place of pure and holy solitude.
Unless you stay there and hoard your peace, and in that, you are so crude.

Because when it is peace that you find in your own special way,
It will do you absolutely no earthly good, if you do not give it away.

For it is divine to restart and renew our lives, especially while we are at rest,
But, it is given to us so that we might pass it along, and help others at best.

Resolve every day to unburden your heart, and let life slow down your harried pace.
For it is in peace and solitude, that you gain strength, to run and to win your own race.

       Jesus left us an example of the ultimate sacrificial life. He showed up down here shrouded in a mysterious birth, lived an obscure life, died a horrific death and will return as the King of Kings. I guess the part that most fascinates me is how He maintained an "attitude of servitude." He came to earth to serve. The King himself, came to serve. He knew enough to do the Fathers' will and by it, portrayed the richness of the kingdom through the highest calling—service.

THE HIGHEST CALLING–SERVICE

My little girl called today, arrested by certain circumstances, that left her frozen.
She spoke longingly of love and about the subtle way that we become the chosen.

Truly loving someone, I said to her, requires a lifetime of selfless service.
And that by doing so, we can say that we have lived, His truly divine purpose.

For it was He himself, that walked down here below, for more than thirty–three years,
To fully introduce the way of service, through a life that was filled with spiritual tears.

The language of love, truly spoken, between the hearts of two people enthralled,
Speaks of a life of services, selflessly rendered, out giving one another, all.

The Holy Book, records a heavenly love, that showed the way of life,
And that every soul was welcome there, and there, there would be no strife.

The only requirement that each person would have to hold and abide,
Is to that everyone we would serve, and that our love, we would not hide.

The highest calling designed by God that each of us should do.
Is to grant by our service, how very much, we love His creation, too.

      Life for humanity has been likened unto the seasons of the year. Truly, as we mature, the eye with which we watch life, changes like the seasons. From the spring to summer, then summer to fall. When the winter of our lives finally arrives, we look back to see how we have faired so far. Spending each season completely is our best hope for this life. To enter those times and not be prepared will surely cause us to miss, the reason for each of the seasons.

SEASONS

As sure as the world turns on its axis, every single day,
Seasons will change and life will too, come whatever may.

To brace ourselves against the change, is to stand against a swelling tide.
We must learn to release our hold on each season, and find peace as we ride.

Learning to flow in peace and harmony, is the only way that we can arrive,
If we are to come to the end of each season, face the King, and not have to ever hide.

Our hearts are our compass, as we traverse through the passageways,
Having it tuned to the true magnetic North, will insure the right way.

Fighting against the flow, will surely bring each of us to an early grave.
But, by allowing God to direct our paths, will, by His wonderful grace, save.

It seems inherent in mankind, that each person must walk their own path.
If they are to arrive at the place, for which they have calculated the math.

At the end of our days, when life has been fully completed,
Our hope is truly, that each of the seasons of our lives, are fully depleted.

Find your own passion and point your heart to accomplish its eternal goal,
For by doing so, you will glorify God, and through Him, regain your mortal soul.

Seasons will change by the hand of Mother Nature herself, on every wave,
So lay aside your pride and your will, lay them away in a grave.

Submit your life to the changing of the times, and try real hard to relax.
Life will continue, and we will live till our end, and that is a natural fact.

But how we arrive and the load that we will have carried thus far,
Will in the end be released, for if it remain, we will not reach the appointed bar.

So, lay it down right where you are at this minute standing, and don't look back.
Jesus is anxious to relieve you of the weight, of that heavy burdensome pack.

There are enough things in life that we cannot get away from already.
Release the load and follow His lead, and try real hard not become to heady.

For, if to God we release all that we try so hard to self–tote.
He will stand before the Father and will gladly give us His eternal vote.

I wonder sometimes, if we can really see true value. Or, are our minds just too clouded to see. The scriptures record that a man found a treasure in a field and went and sold all that he had to purchase the field. I recently have had the pleasure of seeing a field with a great treasure in the hearts of two little boys. I finally saw their real eternal value and wondered if this might not be something that God was trying to say. I had never considered the value of human life in quite this way before. Surely, there is great treasure inside the the hearts of little boys and girls.

THE HEARTS OF LITTLE BOYS AND GIRLS

In all of life and across the land, nothing is as open as the little heart
That belongs to a child, whether boy or girl, and that is where their lives start.

Ever wide open, to the things that we pour in and on their little minds,
Cataloging, filing, shuffling-- trying to get what they see in a straight line.

Their little hearts, are an open receptacle, to the parent that throws down trash.
Not really mindful of the things within, that makes a child kick and thrash.

On the other side of the pendulum's swing, is still what matters most,
That upon those tiny hearts, we bestow the things, that gratify the host.

If we were only keenly aware, of their little hearts ability to grasp,
With love devotion and concern, we would their tiny hands, calmly clasp.

And while we promise still, those things we never intend to keep,
Trust and love, away from their tiny hearts, will always, slowly creep.

By the time that their lives, through our hands, to their little hearts has been fashioned,
What we will have created, will come home again, our own hearts painfully smashin'.

We sit up late at night, and cry out in pain, because they turned out so.
Rarely understanding, that we through negligence, have paved the path they go.

So, listen closely and heed this poetic warning, intended to appeal,
Be careful what you feed a tiny heart, because what you sow, they believe is real.

If we knew the importance of our offspring, I wonder would it change the way we deal with them. Our children are always what we create through our actions more than our words. The weight of words are very powerful, that's for sure. But, imagine for a moment that you are sending a living representative of your gene pool out into the world as an ambassador of your family. What the world will know of you will be carried in your children. I wonder if that is why people say that the apple doesn't fall far from the tree?

THE APPLE AND THE TREE

Throughout this life, and from a lot of angles, I have clearly seen,
The saga of "The Apple from the Tree" and what it really means.

Regardless of what we may ask, think, or even truly believe,
The Law of Reproduction is a fact, and for that, there is no reprieve.

It is all about who we truly are, in spite of our efforts to try and hide,
Our offspring will appear in life, as who we, really, really are inside.

Inside the tree, the beginning root, the trunk and all the branches too,
Will identify, throughout eternity, what our offspring fruits will surely do.

Whether good and healthy, or smeared all over, with a terrible ugly blight,
The fruit of our tree, is in our children, set in the branches, ready for flight.

When from our lives, our homes and our hearts, they prepare to depart,
With them will be going, the truest depths of our own faithful hearts.

They will likewise, carry seeds anew, to start a fresh new branch,
We hopeful, that through tender breeding, have taken away chance.

So, remember always, and especially in your subconscious mind,
That who they are, is what we created, by our own, cookie–cutter design.

    I am sure that you can remember how good it feels to be paid a compliment. Have you ever noticed how a simple kind word can actually turn a life completely around? That warm, fuzzy feeling that comes with a word well spoken can be like the apothecaries ointment to a tender gaping wound. Too often, we fail to say what needs to be said. Life goes blowing by us and we look backward and wish---that we had said more nice things to the ones we love. Oh the soothing effect of a compliment.

A COMPLIMENT

This old world is full of hurt and pain.
Day in and day out, the sting of it, still remains.

How far can a man go, sent on his way in pure ecstatic energy,
Knowing, that focus comes, from a different source of synergy.

Driven by his passion to excel, and to be so very much more,
A compliment can change his course of life, and open once closed doors.

Every person alive, loves to hear the sound of positive sensual vibes,
No one down here would dare not surrender to that kind of "warm" inside.

So, if by chance, you have the opportunity, to bless someone today,
With a sweet word, or a compliment that you might have to say,

Pour it on and let live with love, the holy inspired design,
For we know not what relief, we may bring to a troubled mind.

As we go through life, oftentimes, we somehow acquire a desire to have our own needs met. Everybody has needs, no doubt. Some of those needs are temporarily met by others from time to time. However, all of our deepest needs can only be met by God. Sometimes though, we become selfish in our rush to have our needs met. It is amazing to learn that the best way to receive the answer to our needs, is to supply for others *first*, their needs.

NEEDS

All have needs that are—some real and others red flagging,
Unless they are met somehow, our hearts will always be lagging.

To have our own needs met at every turn, is important to our sanity.
It is not like the clothes we wear, the way we look, no, it is not vanity.

Every living soul, by divine plan, likes to know that they are surely wanted
Not for ego's sake or that by chance, else our hearts might wind up vaunted.

Our hearts cry out for anyone, who will love us where we are.
So by that love, we can be lifted on wings, and travel to the stars.

The high we seek, is not drug induced, or even by it here sustained,
It comes from self worth, and having our needs met, thereby it is maintained.

To believe that we could walk through life, and never need a friend,
Would be completely ludicrous, and prove to be totally wrong in the end.

The lives we live and the people we love, are sent by divine hands,
To help us through and supply our needs, by a helping friendly man.
I need you friend, and that is a fact. And yes, you need me too,
If we are to run this race, and finish the task, that we are sent to do.

So. as we walk down here below, allow me friend, to give real heed,
To your hearts' song, and by my love, help you supply your every need.

Solomon spent a great deal of time doing the research on wisdom. When you read any of the works of Solomon, you can get a real sense of the price he paid for wisdom. As you read Ecclesiastes, you find that he had gotten tired of all of the superficial things of life. He finally understood that only one thing matters in all of life—eternal preparation. He got down to where the rubber met the road. He expounded on the vanity of life. By the time that he winds down from all of his burden of proof, he simply states, 'I am tired of false lives.'

FALSE LIVES

The philosophy, that dictates how we present, is shaky here at best.
It says that who we are, will come shining through, as most of us can attest.

But what is it about the human race, that pushes us to lie,
To swear that we are who we say we are, so help us God or die.

Deception, better dictates, the truest sense of the real us.
We put on a face that suits us well, until we bite the dust.

No one ever sees the real side of us, unless it supplies a need,
But, quickly then, we cover it up, and the fairness of it, we will not heed.

Covered now with false faces, that we have learned to hide behind,
We lie, we hide, we stay aloof and deceive, until we almost lose our mind.

What people see of who we are, is a put–on by which we give,
Showing all of our true colors, is a much too risky way to live.

Find out quickly, who you really are, and live life free of guilt and shame,
For when you leave this planet, the thing left behind, will only be your name.

So, if you have lived your life, and to yourself, you have always been true,
You will be loved and respected, no matter where you go or what you do.

From Gods' first conception of mankind's' presence on the earth, He ordained and spoke into existence, man's special place in His own heart. Every human being is different, and yes, somehow, very much the same. But, into every spirit He created, He placed very unique and wonderful gifts. His plans were that each of us find out what our particular gifts are, develop them and use them to bring glory to Himself. Is your gift laying dormant or, have you discovered and are beginning to develop the gift.

THE GIFT

Very early in time, when mankind was first created,
God placed, in the bosom of His creation, a gift—prorated.

To develop this gift, was Gods' idea, for man to always excel,
To bring forth good fruit, make it to heaven, and to miss a burning hell.

Deep in the chest of every human being, is a wonderful godly passion,
By divine hands, each gift for each of us, He would personally fashion.

At our conception, when life begins, God places those wonderful gifts,
Contending, that through our gifts, we fix the breaches and repair the rifts.

Some are gifted to sing and dance, others to touch and heal,
Some are engineers, lawyers and such, and even farmers in the fields.

The gifts are divine and planted deep, so we must find and develop them.
So that by our gifts, we could bring great honor and glory back to Him.

The things in life that matter most, and raise our holy passions,
Are the things we are called to fulfill, before our final passing.

So ask your self a simple question, when your time in life has come,
What is your gift, what is your passion, and how well was it done.

Dig it up and nurture it. And yes, make it grow so you can fully mature.
For in the end, He will ask of you, how it went, and not with subtle demur.

Our lives down here will be like a great movie script that He truly reads.
Did we listen, did we develop it, and through it all, is He well pleased?

Yes, it is true that in you is a special thing that God has just for you and no one else. We bring Him glory and honor when we recognize our particular flair. As we go through life and exercise our destinies, God is pleased. Some are sent to heal diseases; some to practice law; some to farm; and still others for ministry. There are auto mechanics, steelworkers and the list goes on. How will you be remembered for your time here on earth when your life is over? Is it really all that simple? I think so. All we have to do is leave a good mark—A legacy.

THE MARK–LEGACY

God has commissioned every creature, to fulfill a divine and holy plan.
Given time and space alloted to us, we must leave our mark–every man.

What we do with our time down here, will leave a legacy for those so dear,
So, give some thought to why you are present, and to the Lord draw near.

Finding your calling and your gifts, will surely, mostly your own self please,
But most of all for mankind's sake, your heart behind, is what you are required to leave.

It does not matter how large or small, the trail you leave behind,
So long as you leave a trail for others to follow, and ease their troubled minds.

Each of us truly have something special that God has called us to.
Find your legacy, fulfill His plan, and to the King of Kings, remain ever true.

The things you have inside your heart, are placed by Gods! divine love.
So find your heart, find your calling, and offer it back to God above.

Invoke His blessings upon your life, and follow His plan through,
Be honest with God, and others too, but most of all, to yourself be true.

Life is short at best, when measured by the clock called time,
Apply yourself to find your path, so that a godly legacy, you may leave behind.

The goal you achieve, will to your heart, seem to fall ever so short,
But don't worry over what you leave behind, so long as you at least start.

Lay down track that points to Him, so others by it may arrive,
For God gave you this single life, so you and others can eternally thrive.

Remember now, as you walk through this life, what God has called you to,
Leave behind a legacy of faithfulness, so family and friends, will remember you.

There are all kinds of peace available to God's creation. The trouble is that we pursue peace in the wrong places. We are often found chasing butterflies hoping to capture peace. We look in the strangest places. Some chase finances and others chase romances. Some search for tranquility and others business stability. The truth is that, only one source can provide us with the real deal. Search for a relationship with God and you will find peace.

PEACE

An elusive butterfly, carries the wings of peace,
Catching it and holding on is tough, to say the least.

It flits and flies, looking for a place to land,
Our hope in life, is that it lights on our own two hands.

Going through life, we sometimes get a fleeting peek.
And when it lands, we finally feel that we are now complete.

To hold on tight to the butterfly, can crush end its soft life,
But to enjoy its freedom, we must let it freely fly till it lights.

The peace is great, when at last we learn this lesson,
It only comes from God, and now there is no more guessing.

Peace of heart, peace of mind, and yes even for our souls,
Are what we hope to gain, and never again lose control.

For peace gives rest, to the most troubled and weary life,
Because in the peace, our world will finally, cease from strife.

Follow your heart always to that place of subliminal bliss,
And be real careful that its message you hear, and you do not miss.

Apply yourself to attract the tender butterfly,
And to be true to yourself, you must never, never, lie.

Face each day with a dogged sincere determination,
For in following peace, you can truly reach, your final destination.

Communication has been the bastion of man's existence on the earth. Words have been written and quoted since early times. However, often our hearts cannot convey what we really feel. But there is something very easily understood when we show someone what we are trying to say. It's like teaching a child to ride a bike. You can tell them all you want to. But until they crawl up in the seat for themselves, and feel for themselves, it won't work. So sometimes when you have to say something, try saying it with words not spoken.

WORDS NOT SPOKEN HERE

Love, spoken by the heart, is truly a wonderful thing to behold.
It says, without words, what needs to be said, even when we are old.

Love is indicated by a language, but words are not really spoken,
Because works can lie, deceive and leave our tender hearts, all broken.

The true language of love, is in the acts of service, that for others we provide.
For it is in giving, that love is seen, and by it, cannot possibly hide.

We can talk and use words, until we are completely blue in the face.
Or, we can change the way we love by service, and thus change the pace.

Love, spoken in actions, will reveal our hearts most sincere intent.
And in the face of another, will resound with blissful, peaceful content.

Today, while you still can, pour love into the hearts of those that surround you,
Serve everyone, so that to God and self, you can be forever true.

Every living soul, for real true love, is always looking for humble service.
And for it, everyone will to pain and sorrow, become completely impervious.

So listen with your heart, and apply with your own two hands,
That magic touch, that complete service, does ardently command.

     Fear drives humanity crashing into a corner where we think we have to make choices. Some choose not to deal with the pain or choose something else. Though it is very sad, many people would rather not feel anything than to experience the pain of rejection. The little child that lives within each of us is screaming for love and attention. Meanwhile, the adult in us, pushes the little child down so that we don't feel anything. How very sad. Paralysis takes over the life of anyone that hides behind a wall of fear and of pain. Such is the very existence of the love avoid ant.

THE LOVE AVOIDANT

Let me love you dear, he says to her, with every breath he takes.
Thank you dear, but don't get too near, the pain of love makes me quake.

The tugging to and fro, from the heart that will remain unsure,
Will at long last, fly away and hide from true loves tender allure.

The love avoid ant, in a tug–of–war, is pulled first forward and then back,
Unable to break the bonds that tie, always, our nerves it does wrack.

Love me please, but just a little, I need space to rest my mind.
I am needy some, and for that reason, with love, I do draw a line.

They set the pace and monitor closely the game, and remain ever so aloof.
For to be real is scary at best, and to be totally free, they both need steady proof.

The proof they seek, they know not of, for only time will tell,
If the proof they sought was worth the risk, and did they risk it well.

For who down here can truly know what a day on earth can provide.
So, rather than live in faith and trust in grace, we shudder, run and hide.

The promise that we are given is renewed only day by day,
But, remember always, our hearts are measured by what we do and say.

The love avoid ant protects their turf and controls every situation.
So that through self–preservation, they can monitor and maintain a wholesome reputation.

How sad the life that never sees how wonderful the plan was contrived,
To let them live a life of true love, if in faith and trust they both will abide.

The Scriptures declare that the human heart is desperately wicked and who can know it. A heart that is tempered by hurt or any kind of pain, can turn cold and mean very quickly. God's way requires that you guard your heart, for out of it are the issues of life. Understanding the divine desire to keep our hearts open and always pure, will certainly circumvent the coldness of the human heart.

THE COLDNESS OF THE HUMAN HEART

The Scriptures confirm that the heart of man is a desperately wicked thing,
When crossed by love, life, or circumstances, it does cause a tender sting.

The heart can fill a life with joy, or even a mountain move,
But given wrongs and hurts that come, no one will be soothed.

A heart so true and filled with holy wisdom, will suddenly ugly turn,
If it is supposed, that it was tricked or deceived, and by another burned.

Anger, malice and yes, hate too, will ooze from the bleeding open wound,
Until at last, wrath has been returned, and that is really none too soon.

Who can endure the prison, created by a human heart turned cold.
For the bars created there, will unto its captor, grow very, very old.

If only love so true, as the Father gives, were caught up in our chests,
We would very soon forgive, go our way, and to God leave the rest.

But and alas, the mind attached, to the heavy heart strings broken,
Leave us barren and troubled deep, and grasping tightly to one last token.

Get even it says, for they must surely have to pay it.
For I will not rest or even try to slumber, until my ears hear them say it.

I am sorry for the wrong I did, and here is my blood to prove.
Set me free from this prison, and let my spirit, once again move.

Remember, when, your turn comes, and Deity asks of you one thing,
Have you forgiven those that have hurt you, now let the hallelujahs ring.

For freedom from the prison bars, are granted at His bequest.
So forgive folks always, and to Him alone, leave all the rest.

Like a dog chasing his tail, mankind makes the circle as many times as it takes to get it right. From the cradle to the grave, we continuously trod a well–worn path to Nirvana. Childhood traumas, mid life crises and oh, so much more, sends us ever away from the things that we desire most in life. True love has a way of erasing the pain and thereby steers us into the place of peace. Don't fear the process that takes you to that heavenly place. All of us have at some time declared, "Here I am again."

HERE I AM AGAIN

Here I am again, the place that I once stood as a kid.
The place of peace, before pain, when I ran and hid.

The place of unfeigned love, and of a tender heart.
The place where everyone knows, that happiness first gets its start.

The place of newborn innocence, and of a pure thinking mind,
Before the pain, before the joy, that was quickly left behind.

It has now been years since last I really felt,
A pure and true love, that made my cold heart melt.

A love that says to pain, cease, and now desist.
A love that will no longer, let my heart resist.

A love that says to a troubled heart, let unchained peace arise.
One that conveys the intense feelings, with tender loving eyes.

Here I am again, at the precipice of my liberated release.
The place where my spirit again, does live in blissful peace.

Her voice, her touch, her deep green eyes, and her tender warm emotions,
Driving out utter darkness, and releasing complete fulfilled devotions.

Hardly even knowing, what manner of grace she portrays,
Touching each fear, healing each pain, with glorious tender array.

Here I am again, free to enter into life's main stream,
Anxious to live, anxious to love, and ready to really dream.

The word of God declares the value of just one day. But we are not content with just twenty–four hours at a time. Our desires often reach forward, to "what if" and "one day." Catching a glimpse of the value of today is a difficult task. The trouble contained in one day has often bankrupted mankind, and yet, we howl for tomorrow. Fairly assess the value of today and you will find Nirvana. Don't wish away the present. Live as if you only had today.

IF I ONLY HAD TODAY

If I only had today, and today were all I had,
I would get up with the sun, and spend more time with Dad.

I would listen closely for his warm sweet voice,
Listening for His answers, to my today's life's choice.

I would thank Him for the time, that He had given me today,.
And then I would try to emulate his character, in every possible way.

The next thing, that means so much to me, in this old troubled life,
Is to ensure that my love is stated, to my loving, caring wife.

When I step outside, to begin this day a new,
I would quickly remind her, that to her alone, I am always true.

Next I would take the love and the light, imparted by these two,
Enter the day with eyes wide open, looking for someone else, to bless too.

I would care more deeply than my yesterday's attempt,
Careful not to falter, or to hold anyone in contempt.

Throughout the day, upon others lives, I would pour Him out,
In hopes that one, would truly find, what life really is all about.

It is not the things that we hold, or harbor for our own.
But, that we to others, His great love, has been truly shown.

At the end of the day, I would trace the paths, that I had just run,
Careful to forgive every encounter, where I had failed someone.

Then home to my true love, and again sincerely renew,
How very much that I have loved her, this whole day through.

Then turn again to God, before I do finally slumber,
And thank Him very warmly, for one more day, that He has let me number.

For a country like we live in, Monday's carry a lot of weight. Some people struggle through the weekend praying for Monday, while others dread Monday's arrival. Stressing the importance of every day will eventually free you from Monday's dread. Finding love, both carnal and divine, can bring a fresh breath to every day. Slowing down and smelling the roses that dot our path can relieve us of our stress, even on Monday mornings.

MONDAY MORNINGS

Bright and early, on the first day of a new week,
You arise from your slumber, and into the day you slowly creep.

Monday mornings, they carry an omen for us, everyone.
For some it brings a new beginning, and for others, it is none.

Some folks live just for the weekend, and some of the weekdays ahead,
For some it is the difference between being alive, or just feeling dead.

I have seen Mondays from both sides now, from rainy and blue, to shiny and new.
Now Mondays have a brand—new meaning, since Jesus came shining through.

What once was a terrible burden, and filled with tumultuous grief,
Now brings love, joy and a sweet subtle, heavenly release.

I watch daily, the sun, as it comes up over our mountain home,
And as it happens, I am reminded, that I am never alone.

His grace and His mercy, His love and care, have erased Mondays drear.
No pain or sorrow, mourning, or woe, can enter where He is near.

A haven of rest, His true love will now provide,
Because now on Mondays, I have Him, living inside.

Life's troubles have a great propensity to drag us slowly into a dank, dark hole. If we could but understand the Father's love, we would never fear being broken down. Daddy's love reaches far beyond any trouble that we might encounter down here below. If we could but understand how He is totally in control, we would rest in knowing that everything will always be alright. Somehow, humanity must understand that God's divine intervention will totally release us from being broken down.

BROKEN DOWN

My heart is heavy, my mind is sad, considering what I have seen today.
Have I been deceived, have I missed the mark, or even been led astray.

I was sure this time, of where I was, and to what I was committed,
Until I was confronted by what I had not yet, even actually admitted.

Afraid to talk, afraid to even discuss, the things that we most fear,
Allowing the darkness to draw our hearts, away from what is truly dear.

We carelessly throw peoples' tender hearts, around and around,
Until we have crushed them and trampled them, solidly to the ground.

The thing in life that we cherish most, from those we have come to know,
Is how to be loved unconditionally, and let the rest, all of it, go.

Our heavenly Father, from His ever watchful eye, has seen what matters most,
That we through brokenness and a contrite heart, should seek His holy Ghost.

For until we, in our pride be stripped, and brought to a humble place,
Will never arrive at His holiness, or even finish, our appointed race.

So, broken down sounds real bad, and to most, it will seem so,
But, in the place that we seem stuck, we will remain, and never forward go.

Yield to Him, allow His perfect will to be accomplished in your life.
For in that place, you will be free, and found in you will be no strife.

Every person alive struggles with hard issues that either keep them balanced or causes them to be unbalanced. If only early in life, we could locate the synergies that propel us forward in life and on the right path. Each day that we live, should draw us, like water to the thirsty, into peace, both internal and external. That is how I have determined my souls' search.

MY SOULS' SEARCH

Moved around by emotions and time,
I search my heart for things that rhyme.

Looking inward to discover heads or tails,
In my heart, pierced with nails.

Unbalanced by this old world around me,
I look for true love to just surround me.

Love to deliver from this world of pain.
The dragons in my mind, finally slain.

I watch ever so closely, day in and out,
To find the one love that will pull me out.

In touch or out, cannot be clearly stated.
My thoughts on life, somehow, seem outdated.

I look within and cry without,
Living each day, in dreadful doubt.

Expressions from the heart, struggle to the top,
One voice says "go," another is yelling "stop."

Within the walls of this fleshly man,
A Captain strong is yelling commands.

"Let me out and I will charge,
Defeating fears both small and large."

To release that soldier and lose control,
Frightens and confuses my very soul.

Who in here is right and who is wrong,
What will be my end and what of my song.

Would anyone know in the time of my passing,
What on earth was this man asking.

Only this, that all may finally know,
Locked in each one of us is only one soul.

Liberate it young, and let it nurture and grow,
That, throughout life, it finds total peace as it goes.

      Mankinds' dilemma has been to know himself, truly. At some point in time, every human being will have to answer that age old question. Who am I, really? Certainly, life takes us to places where we question who we are and what are we doing here. By pursuing the divine path, we can obtain value and direction that will surely lead us to that very discovery. God has placed in the heart of every creature, a compass that points us in the right direction, if we will but listen. Follow the gentle urgings of His divine higher power, and there we may find, Who am I, really.

WHO AM I, REALLY

There is a sincere question, that strikes the heart, of every person alive.
Someone, please tell me who I really am, so that I can live and thrive.

Reveal to me my purpose, my talents and my dreams,
Don't leave me in this darkness, to flounder, fear and scream.

Open my mind; Open my heart; that I may truly know,
The path, the road, the right way that I should always go.

Faith says to me move forward, be what your called to be,
Then there is doubt, it yells out, that I shall never see.

I vacillate between winning and losing—starting and stopping,
Trapped between two worlds, either picking up or dropping.

Where in life does a man receive the confidence to excel,
The understanding that it takes to make heaven or just miss Hell.

The balance lies within us all to know, what is right and what is wrong,
It is always found in the heart and is the melody of Loves' sweet song.

Listen closely and you will hear its joyous rhapsody,
Playing softly with both rhyme and reason, Loves' happy parody.

Follow its tune, where ever it may gingerly lead,
Its message, a truly inspired person, will always want to heed.

There are times in our lives when darkness crowds us and tries to smother us. It may be due to the death of a loved one, a broken relationship or even a financial disaster. Often, the dark night seems to last forever. Not so. Time itself is powerful healing tool. No matter what appears to be, as long as there is breath, there is hope. It is not easy to say in the darkness, 'Be still my heart and wait.' Because, in the night time hours, nothing is more dreadful than believing that all is lost. Hold on for the light. Soon gone now will be the darkness.

THE DARKNESS

I arose at every sound, thinking that you would come to me,
It was dark and the night sounds I heard, but I could not see.

Certain that loves allure was strong enough to pull you from your slumber,
Evey hour, on the hour, I was wakened, and by that, time I did number.

Was I mistaken to believe that you could really help someone,
Or was your independence, a settled thing, and my life with you was done.

The night time sounds, felt like cold footsteps across a wooden floor,
It was only the sound of my beating heart, and not you at my open door.

Alone in this tower, I prayed that you would soon come to my rescue,
Assuring me of your sweet love, and chase away the night sadness, too.

The addiction that my love provides, leaves me in an awful pickle,
Because of it I am unsure, and by it, I appear to you as fickle.

Is it wrong to ask of love, to keep me always assured and to confirm,
That I am important, and that I matter, just to comfort and affirm.

My heart to give, wholly and completely, to one I find so true,
Is easily done, if in them, I find that total heart commitment, too.

Words alone can never relieve that longing, lingering question still,
But acts of service done in earnest, always, most surely will.

In order to escape the darkness and to acquire that precious light
We must not surrender to its weight, we must always stand and fight

So know this now and the light will become to you so clear,
Stay close to Him, and in His peace, never surrender to fear.

      There are times in our lives when dark times begin to crowd us out. It may be due to the death of a loved one, a broken relationship or even a financial disaster. Often, the dark night sems to last forever. Not so. Time is a powerful healing tool. No matter what appears to be, as long a there is breath, there is hope. It is not easy to say, in the darkness, be still my heart and wait. Because, in the night time hours, nothing is more dreadful than the loss of love.

LOSS OF LOVE

I arose at every sound, thinking that you would come to me.
It was dark and the night sounds I heard, but I could not see.

Certain that loves allure was strongt enough to pull you from your slumber.
Every hour, on the hour, I awakened, and by that, time I did number.

Was I mistaken to believe that you could need someone.
Or was your independence, a settled thing, and my life with you was done.

The nighttime sounds felt like footsteps across a wooden floor.
Alas, it was only the sound of my beating heart and not you at my door.

Alone in this tower, I prayed that you would come to my rescue,
Assuring me of your sweet love, and chase awaqy the night sadness too.

The addiction that my love provides, leaves me in an awful pickle,
Because of it I am unsure, and thereby, I appear to you as fickle.

Is iot wrong to ask of love, to keep assured and confirm,
That I am important, and that I matter, mjust to comfort and affirm.

My heart to give, wholly and completely, to one I find so true,
Is easily done, if in them, I find that total heart commitment too.

Do for others, mserve without a cause, and always let somwone truly know,
That your love for them is really real, and you think of them, where ever they may go.

      A haven of rest. How wonderful, that given space, we can, in the last hours of every day, find release from the burdens that a day may bring. Remembering always that we are allowed one day at a time, can help us live each new day fully. True relationships can provide for each of us, a safe haven for rest and peace. Life comes at us sometimes at a raging pace and rapes us of our peace. Trusting someone to provide such comfort can be scary for us. But, if we can find such trust and safety, we would not need to worry at all about the last hours.

THE LAST HOURS

All day long, the tug of life, pulls hard on the heart of mortal man,
In and out, and up and down trudging through this barren land.

The load of life weighs ever so heavy at even tide.
So he hurries home to peace and quiet, so he can again, hide.

Into the open arms of love so very, very strong.
To release the load that life has stacked upon him, all day long.

She watches the time and she watches the drive,
Anxious and excited to see her true love arrive.

With an eager heart and arms spread ever so wide,
Welcomes her burdened man back to his haven inside.

He hurries in to tell her, all that has happened to him today,
Anticipating the releasing words of love that she will surely say.

She listens so intently, and hangs precariously on every single word,
Careful to listen and rightly analyze, all that she has clearly heard.

When the time for conversation, has ended in sweet relief,
She has, by her heart, swallowed up all of his nasty grief.

Together now, to their sweet refuge, they will quietly retreat,
And find the loving intimacy, that makes their humble lives so complete.

Into her open arms again, he will gladly, completely pour,
Drawing strength from her soul, slowly, more and more.

Till at last, the night time hours, will once again decline,
Rest comes upon him and released will be his troubled mind.

We go sometimes all the way through life, without ever being true to ourselves and others. Childhood traumas, molestations, loss and a myriad of other stump holes, corral our hearts and trap us in the place that we think is safe. If the truth is really known, we are locked away in a dark dungeon that provides safety, only through isolation. That is not the Divine plan. God intended that we really learn to live. To really truly live, we must not have hidden hearts.

HIDDEN HEARTS

Since early times, the heart of man, has baffled scholars everywhere.
Looking, listening, searching, wondering what is really in there.

Listen to your heart, follow where it leads, obey its every command.
That is the banner raised, where hearts are spoken, ever since time began.

But is it possible to know what lies, within each rising chest?
When following it, we give our all, and do our very best.

And in the end, we will cross that frothy river, to the other side,
Only to stand before Him, and our hearts we will try to hide.

Have we really been completely true, and always done what is right?
Or have we balked and missed the mark, while taking off in fright?

Love turned on and love turned off, like an electric plug,
Causes us to fall asleep, as if we were on a sleeping drug.

The hidden heart, that most of us will never see in the lives of those we so admire,
Is covered up with hurt and pain, and stings us sorely, like a burning fire.

Liberate your heart from the prison, that pain, has for you decided,
Trust in God, lean on Him, bask in the presence of peace that He has provided.

When your heart is hidden and covered for you to defend,
Ask yourself, who to trust, on Him, you can safely depend.

Boy, love is off the map. We live to love, and most of us love to live. How wonderful is a life that awakens before it's too late. A mature love is every soul's wish. Finding that love and nurturing it closely, will ensure that peace will follow. God, in his infinite wisdom, has designed life to take us just on that course. He does not manipulate it, He simply makes it available to whosoever will. So, live life with your eyes wide open, so that you would be right where you are supposed to be when love awakens.

LOVE AWAKENS

For well over half a century, I have been seasoned for one revelation,
To truly discover, before the grave, my own holy destination.

Trained by life, and formed toward perfection, by divine, holy pressure,
Gaging my progress, my length and my love, with a rod of divine measure.

When my season for His grace has finally, fully matured,
True love will finally awaken, of this fact, we have been assured.

For my life, as well as hers, has for this day been directly stirred,
When sleeping, I called, and my voice, she has faintly heard.

But, He will arise with love in His eyes and sweet joy on His face.
Knowing that beside Him always, I have taken my place.

She knows too, that life has seasoned her and brought her thus far,
That together, we can become, who we really, already are.

Divine edit, and ordered to arrive, they find true love real,
When their joy, their lives, their love for each other too, is totally revealed.

Promises are made with heartfelt and sincere devotion,
Finding in each other, the deepest roots of their own emotions.

Awaken my love, and to my side now quickly fly,
For life is short, and without you, I will shortly die.

Are you thirsty? God said to drink of the water of life and you will never thirst again. It is the depth of His love that quenches the parched places in mankind. A lesser drink, and still of great value, is the love between a man and a woman. When love strikes deep in your heart, you can find, that it is much like drinking flavored water on a sunny summer day. With soul ties, we create an ebb and flow that is gratifying beyond measure. Walk slowly, search carefully, and when you have at last found this source, you too, will be drinking from the fountain.

DRINKING FROM THE FOUNTAIN

A man can walk through this life, and can be thirsting for many things.
If he can get a drink as he does, it can make a heavy heart really sing.

Each of us, in our own special way, find ourselves longing for a drink.
Not knowing what it is, that can fill that dryness, that makes our hearts so shrink.

Recently I have found an additional kind of water that fills my heart so full.
When wrapped in her arms, I feel that drawing, drinking, filling pull.

It is hard to explain how one life attached to another, can really truly satisfy.
And more than once as I drink of her, I have had to ask myself exactly why.

What is it about the needs of a man that causes him to parch way down in his soul?
When out of the blue, and unexpected too, water is poured into that hearts dark hole.

So much like God, to allow his creation, the pleasure of His own pure love.
Poured into each of us, without measure, from His heavenly perch above.

Granted by grace to enjoy without fault, the greatness of His human creation,
She being a real part of me, lifts my spirit in an exultant, and holy jubilation.

God created Adam, and from him took a rib, to make the other part of the man.
But, only by finding where Eve is, can Adam become a whole creature again.

The thirsting of our soul for that mate, created to be our one and only,
Will never be quenched, if we don learn to drink, and resolve to never be lonely.

The perpetual thirsting that we do, was intended by grace,
To fill the well and quench the thirst, in only one special place.

The thirsting of my heart, and the very deepest breath of my life.
Can only be filled with my other part, and the true love of my wife.

Wrapped in her tender arms, at the end of a very trying and long day,
I drink from her presence, long and deep, and by it, my burdens are lifted away.

The water of life that will not let you thirst again, Jesus says that we all must drink,
Is much like her love, and from it every day, I swallow long and hard and I think.

How very dry and dehydrated my soul would surely be,
If it weren't for her love, formed like a drink, being poured steadily into me.

Have you ever found love at first sight? Have you ever been so totally moved by the presence of another in such a way as to arrest the last breath you took before you saw them? It can be earth moving, deep down in your spirit. Everything that you thought you knew so well before, suddenly vanishes like smoke in the wind in the presence of that special someone. If you listen close, you can feel the force of nature itself, moving what was once unmovable. That, my friend, is what it feels like to be smitten.

SMITTEN

If you could, through my eyes, see the love that I have for her inside,
You would know the depths of the oceans and the force of the swelling tide.

It is not a love of tender years and fleeting lusts, from an immature man,
But, a stronger love and more mature, one designed by Sovereign hands.

Love itself, in her character portrayed, is more intense than a physical allure,
Yet, her physical beauty in grand display, was totally angelic, that was sure.

In life long lived, I had never been so smitten, by one so fair and true.
If you could see her heart as I do, you would sincerely agree with me too.

The windows to her soul, are eyes of purest blue, full of light and love,
And when you peer into them, she will make your heart soar like a dove.

Her hands, like her heart, are very tender and sharing, pining along with your pain,
She opens her heart, stretches forth her hands, in sincere hope that healing, you regain.

The laugh that she chooses to express her own joys, are infectious and consuming,
Ah, look into her face and see the sincerity, with her heart, there will be no assuming.

She is the sum total, of the epitome of social poise, etiquette and humble grace,
The light in her eyes; the love in her voice; the passion written; are all over her face.

Her life, her character, her loving smile, could never have been written by a poets' prose, For much
like the lovely red flowers, complex and undaunted, she too, is a perfect rose.

The tug at my own heart for her is unsettling, because the pull is so strong,
Loving her and giving all, regardless of popular vote, cannot possibly be wrong.

I count the minutes, hours and the days, till at last I am with her, seeing her eyes raised, Loving her,
holding her, protecting her, for now, forever, and for always.

Human beings are God's only creation that actually makes love, face-to-face. It is a holy
and beautiful thing that we have been given. When appropriately utilized, intimacy of this kind,
can provide an excellent tool to bring two lives together in rapturous wonder. There is, in the act
of making love, a wonder that surely brings a smile to the face of God. It is but a small part of the
total package of blessings that have been bestowed upon mankind. Always remember, God is well
pleased with true loves' holy embrace.

TRUE LOVES' HOLY EMBRACE

When the long shadows of the evening are cast across the skies,
He comes to her side with breathless anticipation, when beside her he lies.

All day long, he has dreamed of this time alone with his true love.
His mind has been full of words and moments with his sweet dove.

With the very last words spoken, that carry away the days stress,
He retires to the bathroom to clean up so as to appear to her as fresh.

He comes softly to her chambers with only one thing on his heart,
Tonight he will show her, how fully she has possessed every part.

As the night swiftly floats away, with the atmosphere of loves sweet song,
He slowly and deftly wiles away hours, so that with her, time becomes long.

As she lays before him, naked and unashamed, he looks deep into her eyes,
He sees before him, his single source for living, and for her, he never denies,

That she alone, has captured the very essence, of his entire earthly life.
Only asking this of her, to remain beside him always, as his loving wife.

He holds her gently, in a holy embrace, certain that tenderness will reward,
The days spent loving and serving her, and trying so very, very hard.

Now, he softly kisses and caresses her soft and youthful, vibrant skin,
Telling her over and over, that she to him, is his very best friend.

While their bodies become entwined in the heated, focused passion,
Their minds drink long and deep, of each others' earthly fashion.

The night is extended beyond the normal bounds, for this night identifies much more,
It makes a statement that the poet, could never have written with deep feelings, before.

With sensitivity for each other, untouched by either, in their lifetimes alone,
They drink deeply from their passion's loving chalice, knowing they are one.

When at last the passion subsides into resolution, unknown as yet to each other,
They fall exhausted to their rest, knowing now that true love has been discovered.

What has mattered most, has, and always will be, face–to–face,
The true meaning of creation, in true love's most holy embrace.

If we could truly be, without the fear of loss, completely honest with one another, I am sure that the places we travel in our minds would not be a surprise to one another. In our minds is our most 'secret you' and oh how sensitive it is to any negative scrutiny. If we could see one anothers dreams, and know the pain that birthing those dreams cost the dreamer, we would become more sensitive to what others may think and feel. We may find by divine edit that we are all traveling in the same direction in our "secret place." It is that private place in each of us, that we are fearful to expose. It is the very place that people must be most sensitive to, always. It is that very spot in which with God, we must have the most sensitivity.

SENSITIVITY

I am sitting here, very early in the new day,
Hoping that soon, inspiration is on the way.

I crave to write what in my mind is truly real,
But, am I ready, its full contents, eager to reveal.

From on the inside, always peering out,
The jumbled mess swirls, with questions and with doubt.

The questions of others, about my journey, would fill a lengthy query,
And to them it must seem that I've lost touch, and of me they grow leery.

I lean not often, to my own understanding,
Otherwise, on my own two feet, I would not be landing.

My mind is raging like a white water river,
And like its cold water over my body, I do so mshiver.

What is this line that my thoughts so closely track?
If I dare go there, can I ever, evr get back?

To dump the contents of my being, out for all to see,
Will by my own undoing, be the total end of me.

Alas, it is so, from deep within, that I must dispel,
Telling the truth to align with heaven and truly miss hell.

All through life, we live unto ourselves for the most part. Have you ever noticed how distant human relationships have become? We are ever reaching inward. It becomes life or death that we find ourselves, get our own Ying and Yang right or just fix our Che. Life was never designed to be about self. Because of selfishness, we go through life and leave a trail of broken bodies that could only be divinely fixed. Still, they were sacrificed for our own advancement. Brethren, these things ought not be. The only hope that mankind has is to keep reaching upward.

REACHING UPWARD

As for me, the roads of the past are strewn with debris,
A long record, written in blood, at sins decree.

To turn now in life and try to direct others trails,
Because of sin, carries no weight, my words would surely fail.

So, of you personally, I would ask nothing at this time,
Except that to God, you would come close and ease your troubled mind.

On the strength of experience in my own life here,
Has to God, caused me personally, to draw very near.

Listen closely while in your youth, you have strong arms,
Draw close to God, cling to Him, evade the impending harm.

The roads of life are strewn with bodies of them that failed,
To reach out fully to open arms that to a cross were nailed.

All in life that you could ever possibly need,
Can be found in the humble, holy Apostles' creed.

A relationship with God, through His holy son, is the only way.
So, keep reaching upward. He will meet you there, is all I can say.

One of the greatest things that we still have left in this country is certain liberties that have been bought and paid for with patriot blood. When we hear the public outcry for the health of our planet, our God–given liberties are not mentioned. We worry about things from the greenhouse to the outhouse; from the ice being gone to the shrinking of the ozone; from oil spills to weight–loss pills. You name it and there is a concern. However, there is one thing left that really must be considered more closely. What about our God ordained liberties?

GODS" ORDAINED LIBERTIES

This thing called liberty, that we in America, abuse so,
Is it really something that we can afford to just let go?

When we begin to count the facets of the liberties in our lives,
Can we, in honesty, afford to allow the loss of even one, and still survive?

Take for instance, the God–given liberty that lets us speak,
As a people, the lack of use or loss of it, makes our nation weak.

Even the liberty to move about within the confines of our planet,
The loss of that liberty to the government, will surely can it.

Liberties that have been paid for by the spilling of patriot blood,
Are lost quickly in the torrents of lethargy, sweeping in like a flood.

The value of a thing is never considered by those not committed,
As long as the dilema of self–preservation is quickly, totally remitted.

As long as it is "not me" who has to pay any kind of toll,
Let us close our eyes to liberty, let the evil darkness roll.

Soon, one liberty that is surrendered, will cause the greatest loss,
It is the liberty that we have in Jesus, paid for on the cross.

We close our eyes and turn our backs on the evil darkness glooming,
Believing falsely, that in this darkness, death for us, will not be looming.

How totally wrong, the apathy toward liberty, that creates a downward trend,
The demise of morality, the destruction of peace, the earth coming to an end.

Hearing God, for the most of us, is an art form that is not easily perfected. You see, there are times when we know that we have heard Him but, we refuse to listen. At other times, He speaks so softly that we don't even hear. And, there are those times when He speaks and we instantly respond. In any case, God is always talking to His children--them that know Him. While He is orchestrating the whole world, He is at the same time, directing the most minute facets of the lives of His kids. Listening ever so intently, have you heard His voice today.

HAVE YOU HEARD HIS VOICE TODAY?

Listen ever so closely and I am sure that you can really hear,
The Masters' voice a callin' ever so soft and oh so very near.

It is not difficult if you will but tune Him in,
It is the quiet place, listening closely that you must begin.

Be very still when any kind of troubled storms assail,
He is ever talking, and in His voice, truth and peace prevail.

Today I lost my keys, and no where I looked, could I find,
Now in a panic, I begin to worry so, I almost lose my mind.

Then all at once, I again remember, He knows everything.
I ask of Him, He tells me where, my heart begins to sing.

He knows before I ask, no matter how tiny may be my need,
His holy spirit listens closely, and never fails to intercede.

So once again I praise Him wholly, I have made the right choice,
I have listened closely, and once again, I heard His still small voice.

Give me strength oh God, to hear it clearly all the time,
And ever upward it will call, "with my spirit" I will ease your mind.

 No doubt, the majority of us have determined that we are living in some of the most troublesome times, ever. There have been many predictions that were foretold that have come to pass. Yet, profoundly, there are a great many predictions yet to be fulfilled. Living in fear of the times ahead has no impact on Gods kids because, in Him, we never have to fear any negative predictions.

PREDICTIONS

Predictions are a look into the future of things as yet to come,
Because so many predictions have come to pass, we are all undone.

There are many more predictions that are for this world of man,
Most are hidden in obscurity, and painfully hard to understand.

Is it not funny though, how the eternal plan was qiuetly placed,
First on papyrus, then on the hearts of the whole human race.

The predictions that were made, foretelling of Gods' eternal plan,
Spoken from the heart of the Father, for the redemption of mortal man.

The promised eventual advent, of the savior of us all,
Specifically designed for those so inclined to heed the Masters call.

It isn't like we have not been forwarned by His holy word,
But genuinely because our hearts are cold, we just have not heard.

In these troubled days, in which we are all still living here,
Predictions of the future made, upon us all, now we truly fear.

So, just as the predictions of the ancient past came true,
So shall those made for our present time, unfold as told, too.

God does not make junk! How many times have you heard that? I wonder if we really do believe it. When you consider how wonderfully and fearfully mankind has been made, you cannot help but notice, "divine intervention." Now, take this creation to the next level. God places within the body of His creation, a part of Himself in the form of a spirit for the express purpose of bringing us to Himself. Knoiwing this, you can see how it truly is a treasure within.

THE TREASURE WITHIN

The heart of man, ever wicked as it sometimes is,
Is ever changing eternally, but only if it is truly His.

Deep inside of us, where the truth will live eternal,
Burns a flame that is set of Him, and that fire is infernal.

Things that are acquired through each lifes, daily journey,
Will give to the victor, an everlasting place in the final tourney.

The crown that is won, will be considered absolute dross,
When compared to the crown worn by Him, on the rugged cross.

Yet, in all of this is a treasure is planted deep within.
His holy spirit, guiding and directing, just to help us win.

Gods' precious spirit, when placed in man, that he be born again.
Provides a glimpse of the future and the treasure buried deep within.

As sons of God, each of us will finally be able to truly see,
What from the very beginning, He has planned for you and me.

Eternal lifde is promised us when His holy work is done.
If only through His holy spirit, we will become as sons.

The treasure now, will finally, eternally be secured,
If our hearts remain in Him, ever steady and oh so pure.

     Love is a language that is often spoken in a multitude of ways. You can say 'I love you,' in a hundred different dialects and still, the message could be garbled to the recipient. When love does come along in your life, would you be able to convey its message clearly to the person of your affections? The depth of feelings and commitment that you have for that special someone, must be fully expressed or the heart will be missed. The next time that you are in the company of your one true love, there will be only one way that she will ever know.

HOW WILL SHE EVER KNOW

When I am around her, and filled with the essence of her love,
How will she ever know that my love for her is sent from above?

As I bathe in her presence, and drink deeply of loves' life,
How will she ever know, how dearly I love her as my wife?

Spending all of my time, watching her every, subtle move,
How will she ever know, that her company puts me in my groove?

Watching her sleep, that restful sleep, that slumber made of peace,
How will she ever know, that in that place, my love for her is released?

When the setting sun is drawing low, and evening is coming on,
How will she ever know, that in her arms, I will always belong?

Her face, her smile, and her loving ways, speaks volumes to my heart,
How will she ever know, that without her love, I would fall apart?

The answer is contained in this simple line of poetic prose,
When in my arms and loving her, she already knows.

Our children and grandchildren are Gods' way of extending our meager lives into the future. As we raise our offspring, we must be very careful to pour only the very best into those thirsty little vessels, that we call kids. Our children will look for a mate that loves like us, looks like us and acts like us. All they know of love. When their time comes to express their true feelings, will they have the right stuff? It is innate in humans to find out exactly how to say, 'I love you.'

HOW TO SAY, I LOVE YOU

As a very little girl, her daddy's heart in her, is completely revealed,
When pouring all that he is, into the shell of a little life to feel.

Her youthful years so swiftly fly, but on dad and his love, she solely depends,
Praying, that when the man of her dreams appears, he, like dad, her heart, defends.

So, as this little girl lives her life, with two beating hearts.
Now she must contrive, to make only one, of the two beating parts.

Because of a dad's love, this child knows, how precious was the single gift,
That was placed within the confines of a frail human chest, to mend a holy rift

A man like dad, with a heart so true, for now must soon be found,
With stoic resolve, she lives life searching, for the 'daddy' love that abounds.

The man she weds and gives her unto, must to the stick measure tall,
To fill the shoes, of a man so rare, as to answer any daddy 'calls.'

Her true loves' character, pure and stature grand, must at least fulfill,
The basic parts, of a fathers' love, and thus satisfy the total bill,

Paid by dad, when he poured his heart, into the frame of his trusted child,
Where he poured all out, the true and complete, the reserved and the wild.

Now comes a man that measures up, somewhat at least, to a degree,
With a love so real and so much like dads, and this she truly sees,

She assures him that her dad she sees, in how he reacts and what he will do.
Finding in him, the need to make the promise, to be ever, always true.

At long last now, the revelation from the fog, begins to finally clear,
She holds his love in great esteem, and bids him kind sir, please remain here.

Even dad, now at last, has found some peace, that he prayed for every single day,
By being dad, loving her alone, her own love now, she can fully convey.
That he is cherished more and more, with each passing, woo,
She can honestly and completely state, how very much, 'I love you.'

Love is not an easy thing to master. Sometimes, it is difficult at best, to comprehend the depth, width and girth of real love. If we can but recognize our life's' mate, we would sell out for that special place in their lives. Being away from the one you love can be terribly heavy at times, regardless of the reason for the separation. However, with a made up mind, each of us can win over an encumbered love.

ENCUMBERED LOVE

To write again of encumbered love, is no task at all.
When I think of her, and the distance between, my heart does quickly fall.

I watch her closely, with a pounding in my chest,
Day in and day out, away from her, I get no rest.

She stays on mind twenty-four and seven.
To be near her at anytime, is almost heaven.

She is kind to me and never cruel or mean,
To watch her smile, and hear her laugh, is a pristine dream.

Her eyes dance, with a warm compassionate flame.
And when I look at her, it is always the same.

The skin that covers her shapely well–balanced torso,
Causes my old tender trembling heart, to beat so.

I count with heaviness, the days till I can again find,
That being with her, I will spend the rest of time.

Ever at her side and so in love, I will always be,
That even the daily hours, I will treat as eternity.

The weight of loves' encumbered truss,
Will, by no means, ever again, affect us.

Volumes have been written about the patience that true love requires. Sometimes, in life, love waits for a very long time to become mature and fully realized. Paul wrote in First Corinthians, chapter thirteen, that love is patient, kind and does not get puffed up. If, for true love, we patiently wait, all of loves' allure will surely be realized. Even with the many facets that love portrays, true love waits.

TRUE LOVE WAITS

In all of life, nothing is as pure, as the singleness of heart.
It is here, in a committed mind, that true love really starts.

The anticipation of true, pure love, makes our minds run wild.
We often become silly and giddy, almost like a young child.

We try to patiently wait, while love grows and matures,
Nothing else in our lives really matters, that is for sure.

We will apply ourselves to the paths that are well—worn,
Praying that true love will come, and never leave us forlorn.

Daily, we pour ourselves into that special someone so very dear,
Missing badly, their presence, when they are not so very near.

But, love is patient and love is kind and waits for its appropriate time.
When at long last, the two embrace, with their bodies, hearts, souls and minds.

Into each others lives, they begin to completely pour themselves out,
Listening closely to their own hearts, ignoring any nagging doubts.

When finally the day comes, love sets itself against the raging storms,
True love, life and happiness, will keep them both from harm.

Waiting for true love and trusting in His divine fate,
Will pay great dividends, if for true love, you honestly wait.

Every mans' woman, has a subtle but sure ritual that she goes though to make herself present as beautiful, to her man. It is genuinely seen during the times of courting. But, a smart woman will continue to do so after they are wed. The ritual for every woman is different and yet the same. From an early morning make over, and back to the bedtime transformation, she is careful to ply her trade in a fashion that keeps love alive. Thus for every woman, there is a ritual of beauty.

THE RITUAL OF BEAUTY

Every day, with the rising of the sun, she begins each day a new,
Conscious of the ritual of beauty, her body, she begins to do.

The first phase, is waking up and assessing last nights toil,
Cautious, that a long and happy life, by that, would not be foiled.

Checking hair, checking breath, and checking closer still,
Watching for those extra pounds, that her love life steals.

Understanding sweetly, that who she is, still matters to him the most,
Knowing that not caring for her body, will soon produce a ghost.

The next step, not so unlike the the one noted at the first,
She will begin the care and attention, that created blissful mirth.

She will now wash, paint, pluck, powder, and oh, so very much more,
To cause her one true love, only her, to love cherish and adore.

By the time that she is finally ready, to face a brand new day,
The transformation from the bed to the job, has erased years away.

She faces each new day with a feeling of enraptured emotion,
Wondering about others gawking, and all the male commotion.

When day is done, to her humble abode, she will again retreat,
She returns once more, reversing the ritual of beauty, making her day complete.

Alone again in her bathroom sanctuary, she quietly retires to undo,
All that the new day had done, to make her look so fresh and new.

Seeming never, to be fully aware of her own heart so pure,
She crawls into bed to see, if in him, she is still secure.

He gathers her close now, late at night, to affirm her rituals' blessing,
Her beauty in his eyes still shines through, without any guessing.

She responds, in her softest voice, to his anxious sensual creep,
Love me darling, for the day was long, and I do so now crave my sleep.

Occasionally, love trips, takes a turn or is somehow tested by life. Sometimes, the daily grind of life, causes us to lose our focus on the things that matter most—the important things. Those times can be very scary for most of us. Given space and time, coupled with patience and communication, love can sensibly be renewed. All it takes is determination and a renewed inspiration.

RENEWED INSPIRATION

This season of death was longer than I had hoped,
Our lives together was now, somehow, on the ropes.

Life has a way of turning like a swelling tide,
Had I said that I do not love, I would have lied.

Today however, marks a decided change of my previous direction,
I saw your face, I held your hand, I made a new love connection.

Missed, you were, as I walked through the Valley of the Shadow of Death.
The pain endured, the loss I felt, were worse than an addiction to Meth.

Now my inspiration has been renewed, and you are the procuring cause,
So, at this juncture, I will belay, think only of you and pause.

Remembering the times, when life was grand, and not so long ago,
Now, ever moving forward and in your care, I will gladly know,

That you do still care about, how I feel and how I live,
So, with open arms and an open heart, all my love, I again give.

Trusting again, in all you are and that what you say is really true,
Once again, I can fly, because my dear, I still love you too.

Mother nature does some really fabulous work during the fall season of the year. It seems that as many people find love in the fall, as they do in the spring. The crisp, fresh mornings bring with them an awakening of the the robust feelings we carry inside. The moderate weather and the promise of a soon coming winter, send people scurrying about with renewed passions. Love itself is wonderful anytime that you can find it. But, nothing can compare to one day in the fall.

ONE DAY IN THE FALL

In the fall of the year, when the leaves of summer start their annual change,
Mother Nature, by divine edit, her total appearance, does softly, rearrange.

It is the time of the year that breeds romance, and so very much more,
Particularly for those couples, whose company, each other adores.

It is such a time, that I now reminisce, and lovingly, tenderly reflect.
Just yesterday, I encountered her presence, with wholehearted respect.

Long since, had been the time, when last we held true loves holy embrace,
But, by the river, and with a full fall armada, we again, were face to face.

The tender looks, the delicate touch, the beauty around so very grand,
Gave way to intimacy and total release, to the woman and the man.

As their hearts, their bodies and their minds, became again as one,
Their emotions, their passions and their thoughts unravel, and are undone.

Swallowed once again, in the rapture that the fall season does bring,
The earth quakes, the lightning flashes, and the birds again will sing.

The pain of the past, is now consumed, by their both renewed confessions,
Of how they feel and what each means, and how true love will make concessions.

As their time draws near, to again return, to the world they have set apart,
Each drinks deeply, one more time, and draw strength from each others heart.

   Love can lift a life from the very depths of despair to the pinnacle of joy. Love, when true, drives away any fears and the darkness associated with it. The kind of companionship that God has ordained for each of us can only be realized by completely selling out to one another. The fire created by young love, must be rekindled over and over again. No fire will burn forever without putting fresh fuel on it. To burn steady, the fire must have oxygen (breath), spark (love), and fuel (substance). Jesus wants us to keep the home fires burning. Only in death, should we see, the last red ember.

THE LAST RED EMBER

For if by rhyme or reason, this sonnet does not ring true,
Consider for a moment longer, what I am trying to say to you.

I have been up and I have been down, more times than I care to count.
But recently, because of love, with golden wings, the sky I can mount.

I have watched her closely for some time now, and know her, I think I do,
The subtle answer to this riddle, is herein contained, just for you.

My days and nights spent with her, always my tender spirit lifts,
My somber moods, from bad to good, does every way, just shift.

When I am loving her, her tender eyes will always reveal,
That what we are going through, is not false, but truly real.

As I carefully cover every inch of her tender body, to map and to remember,
My soul is on fire, and is consumed by her, down to the last red ember.

Though my mind, apart from her, never seems to stray,
Always and forever, on her face, my heart and my mind stays.

Who is this woman, this goddess, wrapped in flesh just for me?
An angel, that was fashioned by Holy hands, way back in eternity.

In your presence and secure in your loving embrace,
I become a real man, and find my rightful place.

The older we become, the more clearly we seem to be able to see. For most of our lives, we are like a spaceship with no gyroscope, no global positioning gear and no directional beacon. Somehow though, our lives still seem to be pointed at 'something.' In retrospect, the road that have traveled this far, seems to clear as our visual acuity awakens. How ironic. How very clear things begin to appear as we start looking backwards.

LOOKING BACKWARDS

In my youth, my behavior was perceived by my dad, as bent and rough.
The childish things that I did, drove my dad to say, "That is enough."

By the time that I had reached my late teens, I had cut quite a trail.
Folks were sure that I would lose it all, I was surely bound for Hell.

I continued on in life somehow, stumbling badly at every turn,
By the way I staggered, it was certain that I was meant to burn.

Throughout the lifetimes of my own kids, ever downward, my life slowly slid.
The mistakes I made were many, and watched closely I was, by the tiny hearts of kids.

Learning of me, the cycle again, into their young lives soon spread,
Each breaking day brought brand new miseries, and painful, woeful dread.

One fine day, as very near the bottom of life, I sickly flopped,
Into my mind, delivered by His sweet voice, a wonderful thought was dropped.

Trust in Me, believe in Me, lean not to your own understanding,
I can help, my yoke is easy. On your own two feet you can be standing.

I was truly humbled that help so strong, could be so very near,
I took Him up on his saving offer, and now there is no fear.

Looking backwards, I can clearly see the help that I had all along,
Seeing His hands guiding my life, has made me spiritually strong.

     The love affair between God and His creation, has been a long running saga. In and out of His love and favor, mankind drifts with the tide. First hot and then cold. Probable causes for the coldness can range anywhere from finances to romances. Regardless, mankind has become lethargic at a very crucial time. God, in His tender mercies is calling out for us to awaken. Can you not hear His plaeding voice asking, "Arise my beloved!"

ARISE MY BELOVED

The day is now very close at hand,
A very troublesome time for mortal man.

On the evening horizon, a terrible shadow looms,
And on the minds of many, mankinds' final doom.

Worry, stress, concern and fear, hangs heavy over earth,
Without a risen savior, mankind will be at its very worst.

Where have we lost sight of Him who holds every heart?
Where, along the mammon hungry path, did we all depart?

It matters not now, whether right or left we have drifted,
What matters most is that our hearts, Satan has surely sifted.

Awaken church, and hear the Masters' tender, tugging voice.
"Awaken while there is still hope, and make the godly choice."

That spiritual man that was once 'holy' alive,
Calls out now with its last breath, "My beloved, arise."

The world has gone really crazy this time. Or, has it finally caught up with its belief system. Our beginning on this planet historically stems from the Middle East. God has always had and always will have, a people that would: Follow Him, Trust Him, and Obey Him. Steadily, this old world is truning back to its roots in the Middle East. Please remember this: God has personally set the whole world in motion and He still controls it, from start to finish.

FROM START TO FINISH

From out of the dust of a far away land,
Both Paradise and Babel, birthed in Iraq, very near Iran.

From this cradle of civilization, sprang both, death and life.
Good vs. evil; Right vs. wrong; days filled with joy and strife.

Out of the Valley of Sumier, flows a lengthy story, spiritually strong.
With a golden history of Gods' chosen people, many generations long.

A history, of His special people, with a glowing testimony grand,
Of His power, love and presence, ever guiding mortal man.

From out of the deserts East, flows a mighty river West,
Riding high on the crest of that river, are some of Gods' very best.

Testimonies abound, of the power and might, of the one true god,
Step for step, He has matched everywhere that His people have trod.

Since those early days when in the East, mankind had its very beginning,
Man has been ever returning to that place, to give account, of a lifetime of sinning.

The battlefield was established very early in mans' civilization.
Now the call goes out for warriors, called from every tongue, tribe and nation.

Prepare yourselves for battle, by resting in His divine, holy favor.
Then watch closely as evil is finally beaten, the moment eternally savored.

Genius is a term that has been loosely applied to deep thinkers. There may be among us, superior thinking, larger brain pans. However, unless that intellect is balanced with the proper amount of sincere recognition of its origin, we may be fooling ourselves. Remember, when we think we know something, we need to remember that all we have is borrowed from a single source. There is nothing new under thew sun. And that my friend, includes true genius.

TRUE GENIUS

Scattered moments of genius,
Surface frequently in our minds.
It's really hard to imagine, what is in us,
Where to look along the path to find,

All that God has created, in the human heart,
The capacity for true love, faith and compassion.
Has for its beginnings a truly spiritual part.
It is the true genius that drives our passions.

Without the spirit of an ever present help,
Especially to keep us on a steady track.
We soon all would falter, with a heartsick yelp,
Crying out in pain, searching for our way back.

When given opportunity, and we try to think life through,
Searching for that place, shrouded in spiritual bliss,
We catch many glimpses of our genius pure and true,
But, if we don't recognize its origin, peace in life we miss.

We are sadly born into this world, as lost as a silver dollar in a trash pile. But wait! There comes a man searching for treasure with a divinely constructed Geiger Counter. The dial is set to find real silver and gold. Buried beneath the trials and tribulations of a life strewn with wrecks, God finds us and brings us into His presence. We are to be cleaned and placed as trophy possessions of the Living God. How wonderful the life that is discovered by Gods' lost and found.

GODS" LOST AND FOUND

For over half a century now, I have plied the pilgrims path.
Left behind from sin's sure curse, a wide, vivid swath of the aftermath.

Living alway for my King, my heart is steadily, toward Him, moving,
And by His grace, my doubts and fears, He is ever soothing.

For the mind of a child, a newborns' gift He gave,
When I asked of Him, He gladly said, 'Yes, I will surely save.

The road has been long and the journey is very often weary,
Without fail, at every turn, He has answered my first query.

Help me please oh sovereign God, I am needing safe direction,
I have lost my way, I cannot see, reveal oh God, my divine election.

The way my son is clearly marked, just follow the trail of red,
For it is the only way to me. It is where I died and bled.

Do not be afraid of the blood stains, along the winding trail,
For it is along that path that your election is finally unveiled.

Trust only in me, for I will steer you, forever homeward bound,
Lean on me with all your heart. I am safe. I will never let you down.

How can I pay the debt I owe, for all the things that you have done,
You owe me nothing, the debts been paid, by my holy, first born son.

Love can lift a life from the depths of dispair to the pinnacle of joy. Love, when true, drives away fear and darkness. The kind of companionship that God has ordained for each of us can only be realized by completely selling out to one another in Him. The fire created by young love must be kindled over and over again. No fire will burn forever. To burn steady, the fire must have oxygen (breath), spark (love), and fuel (substance). Jesus wants us to keep the home fires burning. Only in the very end, should you really see the last red ember.

THE LAST RED EMBER

For if by rhyme or reason, this sonnet does not ring true,
Consider for a moment longer, what I am trying to say to you.

I have been up and I have been down, more times than I care to count.
But recently, because of love, with golden wings, the sky I can mount.

I have watched her closely for some time now, and know her, I think I do,
The subtle answer to this riddle, is herein contained, just for you.

My days and nights spent with her always, my spirit lifts
My sober moods, from bad to good, does every way, just shift.

But, when I am loving her, her tender eyes always reveal,
That what we are going through, is not false but very, very real.

As I carefully cover every inch of her tender body, to map and remember,
My soul is on fire, and is consumed by her, down to the last red ember.

Though my mind apart from her, never seems to stray,
Always and forever, on her face and her heart, my mind always stays.

Who is this woman, this goddess wrapped in flesh, just for me?
An angel, that was fashioned by holy hands, way back in eternity.

In her presence and secure in her loving embrace,
I become a real man, and I finally find my rightful place.

Even love needs rest and solace. The daily stresses of living, can slowly, surely sap every ounce of strength from these mortal bodies and leave destitute and empty. Finding a regular place to rest and rejuvenate is an extremely essential ingredient to a long-term love and life. We must somehow protect what God has given us. Wherever that place is, it must provide a refuge for your spirit and soul. One such place for me has been an isolated cabin on the river.

THE RIVER

There is place near our mountain paradise, that affords us both true rest.
A place removed from the city life, and other things that we so strongly detest.

It is our haven and our refuge, where from our troubles are delivered,
The place that we hold so very close, is our cabin hideaway on the river.

On a deck, and near the water, and perched atop a shaded stream,
We meet, we talk, we laugh and of our futures, we do dream.

All of our troubles, on the flowing water are sincerely gently tossed,
While in this place, with the evening shade and setting sun, all our fears are lost.

When all we know has been rehearsed, we together, will have agreed,
Back inside, with tender love, each others heart, we will calmly heed.

Inside our cabin domain, we tenderly enjoy a light evening meal,
Talking deeply of loves far–reaching arms, and other things so real.

When the whole nights' passion has diminished, into a ravaged rest,
In each others arms and drawing close, we realize in each, what is best.

With a thankful heart for the love we share, we slowly drift into sleep,
Quietly praying and believing that what we now have, we can always keep.

The river now, clothed in utter darkness, slowly flows on down,
Till early morning catches us, and we must return to our little town.

Thankful one more time, for our cabin on old Man River,
Remembering our great time together, we in unison, do shiver.

We hold our breath and hope anew of some better days to come,
When enraptured in loves embrace, at the river, we become as one.

As we go through this life, we will encounter all kinds of people. We must be very careful to recognize the ones that pass through our lives that were sent by divine edit. Oftentimes, we miss our day of visitation. God brings someone through and we never really understand who they are and what they were sent for. My wife was one of those people. Honey, you can relax now, because, I know who you are.

I KNOW WHO YOU ARE

I know who you are now, as you present to the world as a lady.
Your gait is sure, your head is held high, you are not tainted nor shady.

Your spirit screams with passion and vision, now well rehearsed,
Your wounds and your love, you have had to carefully nurse.

You have appeared in the distance as a dimly lit star.
Now you out shine the best of the group, and that by far.

You have withstood the storm, the lightning and the Potters' Wheel,
The express image of Him, in you, is now completely revealed.

I know who you are, as in the spirit, you parade boldly by,
You glow and you dance, from early morning until late nigh'.

Had I not looked or even inquired, I would have missed you by inches,
I know who you really are. You are special—His favorite Princess.

Finding a few true friends in life is the most that we could ask for. True, lifelong friends are hard to come by. When in life, we finally find them, we need to look closely at what God has given us. It has been said that if a person goes through life and has just seven true friends, they are truly blessed. Look around you. I know that for all of us there are in life, a few friendly treasures.

FRIENDLY TREASURES

In all of life, nothing compares to the heart and mind of a true friend.
Someone who knows you well, and stays beside you through the end.

How could you measure, without a divine rule, the depth of a friends love,
When their every thought is for your welfare, surely that is from above.

To measure a true friends heart, is not a difficult task to do,
Get in a lurch, a bind or a jam, watch closely, who comes along side of you.

True love, as we measure it here on the earth, is never as near the heart,
Like the devotion that runs deep in your friend, right from the very start.

The continuous self–sacrifice, provided by a friend, free of any cost,
Will carry you in the hardest times, even if you are totally lost.

Heaven help us to realize, the value of a true and trusted friend,
For in the low places, you can attain new heights from a loving mend.

Covet friends, and keep them true, listen to their heart for you,
For, in times of distress, only a friend can really help you through.

No work about wisdom would be complete if the topic of aging were omitted. As sure as the grave is, for each of us waiting, even it, oftentimes, waits for many years before it comes to collect. It was calendar years that gave Solomon time to reflect. We too, in our promise of threescore and ten, will surely see many things, more clearly in the end.

IN THE END

I once was a young man, but now I am old,
My body that once stayed warm, now stays cold.

When in the morning, my mind is first awake,
I listen closely to my body parts, that now do so ache.

Instead of jumping up, and running headlong, into my day,
I gingerly roll to my side, slowly put my feet on the floor, and stay.

In this position, I count again, and take stock of all my pains,
Trying hard to remember which meds I take so alert, I will remain.

On my feet now and moving ever so slowly along,
I go to the bathroom, and slower still, sit on the throne.

I try real hard to remember the things, today, I have planned to do,
Forgetting some important things, happens to me, more frequently, too.

My body seems to ignore, my most constant mental commands,
I speak to it, but it responds with this shaking in my hands.

Finally, I am dressed and standing near the front door,
I am standing looking, not able to remember what for.

Is this the hope of my final twilight years?
Will my remaining time be filled with awful fears?

There is a place, where from these things, I find an awesome rest,
It is alone with God, with my mental focus on His very best.

The time draws nearer now, for my eternal resting plan,
The time to cross over Jordan's' River, into His anxious, waiting hands.

As life for each of us finally draws to a close, we will leave a stone to mark our passing. It is a given, that every life will end and only the stone will tell where we have been. Remembering the pioneers of yesteryear can serve as a stark reminder of what has been done in our own lives. Hopefully, when the stone is used to mark your passing, you will be remembered for the positive contributions you left behind. Then, maybe they will put your remains in a mountain graveyard.

THE MOUNTAIN GRAVEYARD

There is a place, that is far removed, from our daily life and drear.
It is a place of solitude, where are buried, the older, departed dear.

In Cashes Valley, way back in the Blue Ridge mountains of yesterday,
Are held there, the remains of history, the hard road and the old way.

From the early eighteen hundreds, to a time more recent yet,
Remain stone monuments, to remind us, and never let us forget.

The remains of the old one–room church, still remind the wayfaring pioneer,
Of all the love, the solitude and the presence of God, that still abides here.

The memories of the old days, when wagons plodded down these roads,
Still enlighten modern man, of how the old folks, always pulled their loads.

When I reach my twilight years and long reminisce, of a safer, quieter place,
I will look to the stones, to tell the tale, of those departed, that have run this race.

With much more grace than mortal men may ever truly deserve,
I will remember these, and all my judgments for humanity, I will reserve.

For who among men, may stand with those whose graves show that they have fallen,
And not stand humbly before God, and quietly inquire of their own heavenly calling.

Where, Oh God, will my end be and will others at my burial site, come and see?
Or will it, like those in the Mountain Graveyard, be forgotten for all of eternity.

Only our imaginations can conjure pictures of the eternal. No one really knows what lies beyond Jordan's' banks. The scriptures record that eye has not seen and ear has not heard what wonderful things God has prepared for them that love Him. I have tried real hard to conjure up my own mental pictures. Somehow, my mind seems to come up short. Therefore, I can only imagine.

ONLY IMAGINE

My old, tired, mortal body, now lies slowly rotting in the ground,
My spirit is finally freed from its fleshly prison, where it was earthly bound.

I soar through the heavens, slightly aware of the change,
And care–free as I am, I am naked and not ashamed.

I am quickly drawn to the source of brightest light,
I freely flow towards the peace, I surrender, I do not fight.

There is a warm subtle peace, that floods me as I go,
Its source is not apparent, but somehow, I am sure I know.

My entire earthly life, had been tailored since my birth, and by His hands fashioned,
For this special time, when my spirit from this world, to that world, would be passing.

All the memories of my earthly life, fade with the passing of the stars,
As I journey onward, to that place, where the dearly departed are.

Into His open, waiting arms, with joy unspeakable, I fully plow,
Finally aware of His unconditional love, completely, somehow.

Never again, to fear, doubt or even shed one single tear,
Because, in His presence, forever now, I will be near.

     Old age can be a very dark time for human beings. The signs of aging creep slowly into our lives. For some odd reason, we wake up one day and realize that we are older. Though it did not happen over night, it appeared so. It was at that point in my own life that I began to consider all of my options, including the eventual grave. At first, I was frightened. Then i heard that still small voice. "I will never leave you nor forsake you. I am waiting on your arrival with open hands."

OPEN HANDS

I once was a young man, but now I am old.
My body that once stayed warm, now stays cold.

When in the morning, my mind is the first to awake,
I listen closely to the body parts that now do so ache.

Instead of jumping up and running headlong into my day,
I gingerly roll onto my side, put my feet on the floor and stay.

In this position, I count again, and take stock of all my pains,
Trying to remember which meds I take, to alert, always remain.

On my feet now and moving ever so slowly along,
I go to the bathreoom and sit slower stil, on my porcelain throne.

I try real hard to remember the things that I have planed to do,
Then forgetting the more important things now happens more frequently too.

My body tends to ignore my constant mental commands,
I speak to it, but it responds with this shaking in my hands.

Finally dressed and standing near the front door,
I am caught standing, looking, not remembering what for.

Is this the hope of my final twilight years?
Will my remaining time be filled with awful fears?

There is a place, where from these things I find peaceful rest,
It is alone wih God, my mental focus on His very best.

The time is nearer now, for my eternal resting plan,
The time to cross over, into His anxious, waiting, open hands.

Volumes can and have been written that clearly expound knowledge and wisdom. From the cradle to the grave, mankind has stumbled through this life, always searching for something more, something else, or just something.

There seems to be no way that the right information, in the right amount, can be placed in the frame of a youngster so that throughout life, it can excel in the things of God. Each of us must plow through this life, seemingly alone, while we search for our own souls salvation.

Every person alive, will have to make there own eternal choice. That choice will have to be made while we are a living, breathing soul, down here on the earth.

Only the fool has said in his heart, "There is no God."

ROMANS 9:20